In the Mood for Food

Catherine E. Goin

WestBow Press books may be ordered through booksellers or by contacting:

WestBow Press
A Division of Thomas Nelson & Zondervan
1663 Liberty Drive
Bloomington, IN 47403
www.westbowpress.com
844-714-3454

Because of the dynamic nature of the Internet, any web addresses or links contained in this book may have changed since publication and may no longer be valid. The views expressed in this work are solely those of the author and do not necessarily reflect the views of the publisher, and the publisher hereby disclaims any responsibility for them.

Any people depicted in stock imagery provided by Getty Images are models, and such images are being used for illustrative purposes only.
Certain stock imagery © Getty Images.

Interior Image Credit: Deborah and Michail Heckman

Scripture taken from the New King James Version®. Copyright © 1982 by Thomas Nelson. Used by permission. All rights reserved.

ISBN: 978-1-6642-4366-8 (sc)
ISBN: 978-1-6642-4367-5 (e)

Library of Congress Control Number: 2021917603

Print information available on the last page.

WestBow Press rev. date: 09/15/2021

WESTBOW
PRESS®
A DIVISION OF THOMAS NELSON
& ZONDERVAN

Dedicated to:

———◆━✕━◆———

Russell Goin, my brother who makes my books possible
Deborah Heckman without whom I couldn't have done this book
Dr. David Goldstein who encourages me to write
Pastor Rick Warren, the author of "the Daniel Plan", a huge inspiration for this book

Cover and Back cover photo: unknown photographer
Photographs in the interior: Michael Heckman, Deborah Heckman

Other Books:

━━━━◆━▷◆◁━◆━━━━

"Mercy, Lord, Mercy", "Broken-hearted Schizophrenic", "Spirit of a Sound Mind," "CAT Meows 2", "Changes Deranges". "goin, goin, gone"

Before the Fall…. Genesis 1: 29-31

[29]….And God said, "See, I have given you every herb that yields seed which is on the face of all the earth, and every tree whose fruit yields seed: to you it shall be for food.

[30]…Also, to every beast of the earth, to every bird of the air, and to every living thing that creeps upon the earth, wherein there is life, I have given green herb for food, and it was so.

[31]…Then God saw everything that He had made, and indeed, it was very good. ….

After the Fall: Genesis 9:3- 4

[3]…Every moving thing that lives shall be food for you: even as the green herbs….

Table of Contents

———◆»✕«◆———

PART 1…

This book is about food, my opinion about food (the necessity of good food for human beings and also other creatures) and hopefully will impart to you my feelings that we need to cook for good health, a healthy brain and mind and an active, attractive body.

1. Traits Which Appeal to Me 1
2. In God I Trust 2
3. On Fat! 4
4. Donald Duck! 6
5. Mood Food 7
6. A Halloween Repast. Will it Be My Last? 9
7. Fixing Dinner 11
8. Haiku is a Treat! 13
9. Food for Your Mood 15
10. The Carnivorous Mushrooms 17
11. Food and Water to Drink Help Ones' Brain to Think 19
12. When I Sing Happy 21
13. Food Has the Power to Heal 23
14. When Your Stomach is Hollow 24

Traits Which Appeal to Me

As for cats…..I adore them….they're so funny
Their philosophy suits me:

> Having fun and coming in at night
> Chasing balls and sticks
> Chewing catnip
> Curling up on a pillow for a nap
> Communicating when the mood hits

All are traits which appeal to me
That's why I like cats, you see!

As this book begins I'd like to introduce myself. My name is Catherine E. Goin (betsy) which is way too sophisticated for a little, old lady like me, so I am writing in my new persona….Cat. E. Goin….which more accurately sums up my current personality. I attempt not to be too judgemental and catty but the real me seems to always surface.

I began writing about 15 years ago, love it immensely and have self-published 6 books as no publishing house or agent seems interested. My true love is poetry. Before writing I painted for about 50-55 years, mainly in oils and acrylics, but I dearly love drawing. I stopped painting when I took up writing because it seemed that what was necessary for me to be say in the art world had been said and I had said through painting what I couldn't express in my words. But lately the urge to draw has resurfaced.

My other true love is music. After studying piano in high school and college I gave it up when I began to fly as a piano was too expensive and big for a financially strapped young FA living in small apartments. To further aggravate the matter I lived in 17 apartments in 6 different cities on the Mainland and Hawaii in 10 years. So in my 50's I took up playing the flute because it was small which I gave up after 25 years as my right side was completely and nearly incapacitated. I took up the guitar and mandolin and recently purchased a Native American flute. Singing is fun but my voice is abysmal.

I live with my brother and we like to sit on the deck and watch the birds and squirrels and rabbits and occasional fox, groundhog, and deer. About once a year a bear comes through the back yard and destroys the bird-feeder, trying to get the seed. This year (July 17, 2021) he came through but there was no food as Russell emptied the bird feeder because the black birds were eating everything and driving away the other birds. The bear knocked over the bird feeder, left a big puddle of poop in Azmir's yard and left. We almost feel guilty there was no food for him.

In God I Trust

Oh, little dust mote, on a sunbeam you float
In front of my eyes! Are you really so wise
That you know what my doctor will say
To help me chase the blues away?

"Miss Goin, you seem depressed!
Not only that but your mind seems stressed!
We need to find you something to do …..New!
Something interesting to do…to occupy your soul.
I suggest you learn to drive
And in the process manage to stay alive.
Driving is interesting and ought
Help focus your thoughts.
I realize, you know, that the blues
Are not humorous nor are they glamourous.
You should not sit and think about problems.
The best way to solve them is to occupy your mind
With new endeavors of a positive kind.
Besides you will need to get to the airport
And in the country that is the only means of transport.
Driving is also fun….essential to be done.
So learn to drive and get a car….
It will get you here and 'thar."

Oh dear, oh dear, my path is clear
Drive I must! In God I trust!
"And cooking too," he said, "is good to do."

So began a new adventure, one among many. I was suffering from a 'serious brain dis-ease." There were many challenges to be faced and this obviously was one among many, the first to be sure. My mother rose to the occasion, took our lives and her car in her hands and decided she would teach me to drive. I was 32 years old and had never been behind the wheel of a car and had never had even the slightest desire to drive. Living in cities and walking everywhere or taking public transportation had been fun. But being ever up to new challenges I gritted my teeth, got my drivers' license and started on the path to 'driver-hood.' This endeavor curdled my blood but even I realized that the only way to keep my job was to be able to drive, get a car and drive to Dulles International Airport. I had three months to learn to drive and get a car. All I knew was to stay between the lines, observe the speed limit and not hit any other car/s or pedestrians. My nerves were stretched to their maximum. I was told the French way to drive is not to hit the car in front of you.

After many blood-curdling adventures while learning to drive I got into the car with a policeman and took off. He told me where to go and what to do which I dutifully did and to my utter amazement I met his approval and passed the driving test….and got a drivers' license. Then Mom and I went to the Nash dealership in Manassas and got my first car, a burgundy-purple Gremlin which I named Mar-gar-ita-furr. I found a bumper-sticker which said "Beam me up, Scottie" and took off.

My first solo excursion was down route 66 to Tysons' Corners to go shopping. I was no longer dying from anorexia and needed some new clothes to fit the 'new me.' When I managed to merge onto 495 from 66 and got into the right lane I was so frightened my knees were shaking and I nearly stopped right in the middle of the highway with traffic whizzing by on all sides. However, all is well that ends well, and I got to the parking lot and merrily went into Nordstrom's for my shopping spree. I finished shopping, had some coffee, watched people (one of my favorite pastimes) and then headed back to Warrenton….an amazing day I will never forget!

On Fat!

Oh to be skinny! Oh to be thin!
Obese is not 'in.'
Rolls of fat cascading down
Evoke disgust, provoke a frown!
Most displeasing to the eye….lose them! Try!
To be a stick is my desire! To be flat, not fat!
Cellulite, a memory! To be flat, not fat!
Many people take disgusting drugs.
Doctors dispense them with nary a shrug.
Will your heart stop as on the ground you drop?
As on the ground you plop?
You are sick and are not able to work the following day,
Nor can you play.
The heart, the brain, diabetes too all bedevil you
If you are not stable, if you are not able
To cut back on food, to stablilize your mood.
Dear God! From the depths of my heart I pray
Take this disgusting fat awayl
I pray, "take this disgusting fat away!
Do I seem obsessive? Or over-reactive?
Well, for a fact I am.

My doctors have been concerned that I keep my weight in the normal range. Considering I have gone from severely anorexic and the doctor saying "Miss Goin, you can either eat or die!" to the next doctor saying "Miss Goin, you must lose 30 pounds which you have gained from quitting smoking." Not only did my clothes not fit, but test results showed I was pre-diabetic and had an irregular heart rhythm.

What does one do? Diets are silly in my opinion and do not seem to work in the long run. So I started attending Weight Watchers and within a year had lost about 20 pounds. Over the next 20 years my weight was down around 35 pounds. The doctors and I were happy. I felt better, looked better, my blood was normal and my blood pressure was down, sometimes normal. My heart was normal. Yeah!

In case you think I am obsessive I am. For 45 years when I went to the doctors they had me step on the scale. What really surprised me was that they expected me to tell the truth about the number on the scale and I did. That was different from when I was a FA and had to weigh. Then the supervisor looked over ones' shoulder and recorded ones' weight…not expecting us to tell the truth about our weight.

I certainly don't expect the government, the food industry and the insurance companies to care about helping our population to be healthy. They are all making tons of money off of unhealthy, sickly and increasingly unattractive people. They literally prey on young people and the poor….who are becoming sicker and fatter which is not normal. SAD! And don't get me started on what our 'factory farming' of animals and the production of corn, wheat and soy (largely subsidized by the government) is doing to our health and to our home planet, Earth.

How did I manage to lose this weight?

1. almost no processed or fast foods
2. no white (including almost no grains or sugar)
3. diet sodas on rare occasions
4. lots of movement including walking, yoga, tai-chi, kayaking, dance and whatever else appealed to me including weight training and cardio machines.

I keep a journal and meditate (which calms me, giving me the time to reflect on what I am doing and whatever is on my mind at the time.) And as I am a follower of the Way of Christ I realize my body is the home of the Holy Spirit and is to be treated with care, integrity, respect and dignity.

As most of us desire to be healthy, mobile, attractive and able to participate in fun and adventures with our family and friends it is important to care for our bodies, minds and spirits…which leads us to the subject of this book…the care and feeding of our bodies which includes cooking, the preparation of food and entertaining.

Donald Duck!

Donald Duck brings me luck as he sits upon my desk.
His blue-colored belly is not repressed.
He smiles with glee inspiring me to laugh with joy!
What a boy!
His eyes gleam and beam…they seem sincere, not drear.

"Oh Donald," I ask, "help me finish my task
Of writing this book about how to cook,
From one knowing nothing about turkey and stuffing!
Encourage me still if you will!
Help me to hurry, to scurry from stove to sink.
Help me to think about what to drink
At the party! What is hearty?

Learning to cook! It seems I need a book and a recipe. My brother on the other hand has learned to rely on himself throwing things together if he wants dinner. I am getting better but still have a long way to go. It takes me hours and days to ponder what to eat. After figuring what I want to fix it is necessary to go to the grocery store to find the ingredients, and having limited money and lots of time, I go from one store to another finding the cheapest ingredients which are non-GMO, don't have lots of artificial ingredients, and are real food. As Dr. Hyman said on one of his shows about cooking to maintain health and a good weight, "If it doesn't rot, don't eat it!" That makes sense to me.

Fortunately I live in one of the wealthiest counties in the USA and have access to lots of good food stores and farmers. Unlike many 'food deserts' if food is available it is available here. As I am finding out, food here is becoming as expensive as it was when I was flying to Europe. Unfortunately the quality is often lacking. Americans for the most part have abysmal eating habits and it shows up in the fact that possibly 75% of us are from slightly overweight to morbidly obese. Our weight and health are probably the worst in the Western industrialized world…probably related to our obsession with processed foods, fast foods, sugar and soda, and eating constantly and huge portions. The older I get it becomes apparent that the majority of Americans don't move. Movement is essential to good health. Getting outdoors is even more important, if that is possible. Not only does it contribute to one's good health but being involved with Nature and its' creatures and plant life is good for ones' ability to deal with depression and also to get the sunlight essential to well-being.

Anyway I will work on my book about learning to cook and doing so as inexpensively as possible while still getting quality food. It is essential and fun. In the process of becoming 'un-vegan, vegetarian' I have discovered a great love of 'cheese if you please' and 'make it meat, not sweet.' If one must have it sweet consider honey and not a lot. And for the sake of ones' soul and body forget low-fat. That's not where it's at!

Mood Food

Food is the enemy! Why is that?

Does it make one fat?

It never occurred that the reason might be me!

Eating too much of food

Hoping to improve my mood

Hoping to give a burst of energy, you see!

And in the process eating junk:

    Sugar, white, processed gunk

Obsessed with trash---that---makes one fat!

Then the government and food industry

Decided that lots of grain would ease the pain

And in the process make us people gain

So much we became obese, leading to :

    Heart attack and strokes and diabe-s-ity --Yes indeedy!

Fed us 'food-like substances---not food

And in the process became rich at our expense---

HOW RUDE!

This slop caused our brains to stop, we couldn't think

But we could drink lots of soda and alcohol

And that's not all---plenty of drugs to deaden the pain

From all the weight we gained.

But finally I became aware that I care

And started to eat 'fat', meat and cheese

Which brought me mental ease

And eggs because they tasted good, bringing satiety

Setting me free from gorging which is enlarging

And then I realized to my surprise that if I cooked

I looked better! Not fatter!

So this book is about how I learned to cook…

Hopefully not getting burnt or hurt

And to entertain, to enjoy food!

In the Mood for Food!

So now I am sleek and thin because I am happy within!

After self-publishing 6 books it became apparent a cook book was in order. I like to entertain and realize that most people like to eat…not only eat but they want good food. I am now in great old age learning to cook, to keep my weight down and to make others happy, which seems to be part and parcel of the human condition.

Another reason for writing this book is because it seems that all writers, at least of the feminine persuasion, write a cook book….sort of a 'rite of passage.' So I decided to bite the bullet and join the ranks of the would- be chefs of the world and produce a book which would not only help me learn to cook tastefully and inexpensively if possible, and in the process help all of the others who have not learned to cook for themselves, families and friends.

Looking around in the year 2020 it seems most people, of all types, are anywhere from slightly overweight to morbidly obese which is appalling, affecting not only their appearance but their health both physical and mental. Physical is obvious: heart attacks, strokes, painful joints, diabetes,etc. Mental is more subtle, having to do with appearance and disturbances of the brain. In the realm of brain dis-ease are not only severe brain disease like bi-polar, schizophrenia, autism but also mental disturbances like anxiety, PTS, varying degrees of depression, etc.

Excess weight is affecting us not only physically and mentally but also limiting our mobility. How did this happen? And lest you think I am being judgemental, to be truthful I have suffered from nearly every type of eating disorder, from acute anorexia to overweight and discomfort. In fact my doctor finally said I needed to get rid of the extra poundage if I wanted to be happy and healthy. Enough is Enough!

How to do this puzzled me. I was active and a vegan so you would think everything would be hunky-dory. But it wasn't. I didn't eat animal or flesh products or dairy or eggs. I was always hungry and it seemed I was always eating.,,three meals a day plus 2 snacks and sometimes more. I felt awful! What a dismal fate the government and food industry had advocated for me/us.

But in 2018 after suffering a fractured spine and a right hip which had a 'severe degenerative hip disease due to injury' following 2 falls I had a total right hip replacement and I spent 9 or 10 days in a wheelchair at Encompass Rehabilitation Hospital where I was fed acceptable amounts of protein of the animal/fish variety, little grain, limited sugar.…reasonable amounts and no seconds. Sitting in my wheelchair staring at the bare walls and thinking (when not doing physical therapy) I realized if I wanted to heal I would have to eat flesh and other such products or my hip would never heal.…so my habits changed!

Now, 2 years and half later, my hip is working and I am slowly but surely walking more and doing limited yoga again. I have lost an additional 16 pounds, my blood pressure is reasonable, and my heart aryhtmia is under control.

About this time the paleo/pegan approach to eating was in full swing and by following it I was almost never hungry. BUT: I realized I would need to learn to cook. Being a woman of "steely determination" I sat out to conquer the kitchen. Enter Dr. Mark Hyman, David Jackson of Food Over 50 fame, and Sue Ward, a nutritionist at Sanoviv Medical Center in Rosarita, Mexico who helped me understand about food. They are all food wizards in my opinion. Generally following their advice and listening to my body I entered the kitchen, sharp knife in hand and began to chop, chop, chop. Being single and retired I had the time to do what needed to be done to cook for myself, my brother and friends. Most people do not have the luxury of this much free time, so it seemed a good idea to not only learn to cook myself but to write about what I have learned. Also to help people learn how to cook as inexpensively as possible. Food is expensive and most likely going to become even more so.

Here goes with my learning/teaching experiment which hopefully is beneficial to me, you all and your families and friends.

A Halloween Repast. Will it Be My Last?

Butter, butter with which to grease the pan
So I can make cornbread on which to spread
More butter, to go with my beef kebobs on a stick.
We can eat the beef and veggies
And lick our lips because the taste is so swell....
Well!
The tomato bisque was a chore for to make
The spirit soar and also to be tasteful
While not being wasteful.
The salad greens with onions, olives and vinaigrette
Were wonderful also making our spirits soar.
Wine and sparkling water oughter' help one rest and digest,
With conversation interesting and replete
Making the dinner complete.
Not to mention dessert, a touch of cheese if you please
And an after dinner a liquor to end the repast.
We don't need more, this will last.
Will it be my last?

That was the plan for Halloween dinner for five. I found the coolest cast iron cornbread pan at the Fauquier Community Food Bank Thrift Store which has dancing bears in which to prepare the cornbread mixture. Hopefully the bears will dance for dinner. It is not a Griswold but probably at least 50 years old. I fell in love with it and then prepared dinner around it. With the five of us at dinner there should be lots of laughter and sparkling conversation to go with the wine and sparkling water...I am the only one who has to be content with sparkling water because my doctor said alcohol is 'toxic to my brain.' Fortunately no one either notices or cares and I can go merrily about serving dinner in peace while everyone else giggles and laughs.

As a first class FA for nearly 40 years I do know how to serve dinner. In fact when flying to Europe on the Boeing 767 which had only 9 passengers in first class, it was expected that three of us (the galley slave, the aisle attendant and the purser) would complete the service in three hours. At the end of the three hours all three of us were exhausted and the passengers were full and happy. Then the passengers watched a movie and went to sleep. I no longer smoked so was satisfied with sitting on my jump seat, savoring a cup of steaming coffee with crème. Ah, the sweet joys of life!

I have learned to serve (and eat) adequate portions but not large. That way everyone can try everything on the menu which appeals to them and not get stuffed. One thing important when entertaining is to ascertain what, if any, allergies the guests might have. I, for one, am allergic to shellfish. Every time I have had shellfish it meant a visit to the local emergency room. Pity! To never again have crab cakes is a tragedy to my mind.

Also I learned to clean as I go. Airplane galleys are small and require infinite attention to orderliness which is also important in the kitchen in my brothers' home which is small. I can disappear from the dinner table because usually everyone is having such a good time they don't notice I'm gone. Nothing is more disconcerting to me than a messy galley or kitchen. It's also important to clear empty dishes from before the guests. Nothing annoys me more than sitting with a dirty, empty dish in front of me.

My brother is one of the slowest eaters I have ever encountered but seems to enjoy what is placed in front of him...what I am learning to cook.

Planning the menu is of the utmost importance and usually takes me about a week to decide. Then one must choose the recipes and shop for food which is affordable. Since I am retired and have more time than most people it is possible to shop around for the best deals. I live in an affluent area where there are 4 supermarkets in town, a Wal-Mart and another super-market in a 15 minute drive. By looking around I find that cooking is affordable, more so than eating out. It is also important to read labels so that the food is tasty, healthy and 'real' food, not loaded with artificial chemicals which are passed off as 'food.' It seems that then people don't eat as much, stay thinner and healthier.

I have noticed when I serve good food for dinner and wine and liquors are served...when the food and company are so much fun that drinking is kept to safe amounts there is no need to worry about drunk drivers and drunk driving....especially as coffee is served after dinner.

Fixing Dinner

Fixing dinner used to be a chore
And what is more…eating wasn't fun
And then there were dishes to be done.
The calories counted up, filling one with remorse
I had trouble with my weight, of course
But since cooking it's not so tough
To keep my weight and health good enough
Sugar had to mostly go and other 'white' foods,
Also heavily processed and fast foods
Which upset and trouble ones' mood.
"Food is medicine" Hippocrates said, 'if you would
Prefer not to be early dead.'
And what is more (a radical thought): one ought to move
Not laze around which is not sound in excess
Making ones' life a mess.
I would have you know God did not intend it so.
Your brain is yelling "My body is swelling."
That's not good so if you would
Eat better food your mood would improve
Your mind and body would groove

The subjects of food and entertaining and weight and meditation fascinate me endlessly. My whole career was built around them in one way or another…how to do them all, stay healthy and enjoy good company and good conversation. One thing for sure is that I despise fast food. The taste and texture is awful, there are almost no nutrients and it is meant to be gobbled in a hurry with little attention to gracious dining. Half the time it seems fast food is meant to be wolfed down in a car. The portion sizes are abominable. No wonder 75% of Americans are overweight, not to mention that we are exporting our abysmal eating habits all over the world and other people of other nations are beginning to look like us. It has gotten so bad that when one sees a normal size person one thinks they are underweight, perhaps even anorexic. How sad!

And with covid all over the world it seems that stress, depression, anxiety and suicide are on the upswing. Not to mention that most people do not get enough exercise and sunlight to stay healthy.

Which brings me to the subject of meditation. Even WW advocates one meditate to help quiet the mind so as not to be subject to excessive cravings and mindless eating. These cravings are usually for unhealthy fats, sugar and sodas and immoderate quantities of alcohol and food heavy in salt. When meditation is practiced it quiets the mind, lessening stress and leads to not requiring unneeded food. We, as human beings, don't require lots of food, certainly not three heavy meals a day plus snacks.

We are all unique and our bodies function differently in some ways, and different ways of eating are called for. For years I was a vegan/vegetarian and overweight. When I spent 10 days in a wheelchair after hip replacement due to injury in a rehabilitation hospital where they served moderate amounts of meat, fish, cheese and eggs the doctor and I realized if I wanted my body to heal, my habits would have to change and especially as an old person I needed more protein. So entered meat, eggs, fish, good fat and cheese into my diet. Sixteen pounds evaporated, no longer is there excess poundage and keeping the weight off is not difficult as hunger is no more a part and parcel of life. On most days I get three hours at least of exercise and movement like the three hours of physical and occupational therapy I received daily at the hospital rehabilitation center. Cooking is a necessity. It is fun, the food tastes good and large quantities are not required.

And most importantly to my mind is that meditation and/or mindfulness is absolutely essential.

Haiku is a Treat!

Haiku is a treat
I repeat, it gives one a thrill
Up the spine…a chill

Five..seven… five, divine
Reside in the mind….sublime
Until the mind reels

Less space do I take
On this small, blue world of ours
Flying through the sky.

Haiku in all its' glory
Is here to tell its' story
To all, big and small.

The food one devours
Envelops the brain in bliss
Fast food does not this.

It appears to me
That if one would be quite well
Don't eat it at all.

It tells a story
In few less words of course
It shows no remorse

And feels such delight
When there is much less of me
To propel through space.

Meditation slows
And tells us to eat with grace
Through our time and space.

Please say a prayer
Thanking God for His 'soul food'….
Improving our mood.

It has no value
Other than to make one sick
And weigh more….soul sore/

Fast food and sugar are the specific causes of my present ire. They do more harm to the human body and brain, in my opinion, than almost anything besides white flour and the other 'whites.' I don't know which is worse…probably sugar which seems to be more addictive than heroin according to some of what I have read. Usually I don't eat sugar but because of the election, covid and other stressors I have been indulging my sweet tooth which for the past 20 years or so has been largely non-existent. However, this past week I have been stressed to the point of eating sweets and putting cappuccino mixed in with my coffee. I woke up this morning, stepped on the scale and nearly fainted. There were three extra pounds which may not seem like a lot but for someone who is only 5'1" tall it makes a huge difference in the way one feels and the way clothes fit. Not only that but I was shaky and sort of tempermental which is unusual for me.

So back to sugar…maybe a piece of fruitcake for Christmas. My mother made a wonderful fruitcake for years and if I can find the recipe I will include it in my book. Hopefully the dried fruit ingredients are still available. It will probably cost $50-$75 to make from scratch and should be challenging as I have never made a cake before. Partially because cake turns me off. On second thought perhaps I will buy Claxtons' fruit cake which is very good and inexpensive, if it is still on the market at Christmas time.

Back to the crème in my coffee…or rather 'half-and-half.' Another big factor in gaining weight as a nation is that we are being told that fat is bad for us. Instead we should eat lots of grains, pastas, etc. It's bad enough for adults but what it is doing to our children and young people is nothing less than criminal. Not only is the extra weight detrimental to the health of our hearts and leads to diabetes, but is unattractive, often leading to depression. We are probably the wealthiest people in the history of the world, but millions and millions of our citizens suffer from depression and anxiety which is possibly a factor in the rising, sickening number of youngsters committing suicide. That is depression carried to the extreme, affecting the brain.

As for fast food…..what can I say? It has no nutrients to speak of, no real food value and is meant to be gobbled down with no emphasis on fine dining. It also doesn't taste good.

I want to emphasize the importance of thanking God by saying grace, thanking Him for our daily food which many throughout the world are lacking. Eating with others is a great pleasure if possible. Conversation and laughter are a treat, enhanced by the enjoyment of well-prepared and presented food. It takes time but is meditative and creative. It is also something to teach your children if you should be so lucky as to have some. Why feed your pets better food than your children?

Squeeze in time to cook…the theme of my book. I am learning along with you all…men, women, boys and girls. Have fun and when the preparations are done, sit down and dine either alone if necessary or in the company of others if friends and family are around.

Food for Your Mood

Food for your mood is good if you would cook
Perhaps using a book
Your brain will say thanks, and you'll take fat off your shanks
You'll be healthy and slim and happy within.
Food goes to the gut whose job is to digest nutrients
Which power your body and soul….makes sense.
Leading to the end result which doesn't insult well-being
And leads to the wealth of a happy brain which sings this refrain"
"Thanks to you I give guidance to the mind/body work
And don't shirk your appearance and as Snoopy would say,
"Dance away today!"

Why do I want to change? Why do I want to change? How will I change?

Here goes: if I don't change the chances are good I will end up tragically like my mother and father. It will take a real effort on part, and hopefully will impact my brother and friends as well. The end result will possibly affect us all mentally, spiritually, physically and emotionally. The hope is that it will give us the vitality and heart to do what God purposes for us to do. My belief is that God has a purpose for each and every one of us, giving meaning to our lives and will enable us to be an inspiration to others.

My goal is to bring about Gods' purpose for my life as best I can: 1….The Saturday morning vigil in Warrenton for Black Lives Matter, vigils which have been going on since early Summer. 2….I am writing my first book about food hoping it will help others learn to cook as I learn to cook. Cooking is one of the most fun and creative outlets, good for the brain and good for the body. I am writing and doing these changes to help myself and others by imparting what I am learning about brain and mental health. 3…I am getting at least 3-4 hours of movement a day which includes 2 hours of walking meditation. In these deadly times the diminution of stress is of paramount importance. 4….Hopefully healthier people will have the patience and vitality to work toward the restoration of our weakened democracy which although not perfect is, to paraphrase Winston Churchill, the best there is. They will also work towards a safer environment and climate. We don't want hundreds of thousands of souls dying needlessly from the deadly covid-19 virus. Everyone should have basic medical care and if you want more you can buy it if you can afford it. Many of the people who don't want others to have this basic are costing the government, insurance companies and me a fortune with their demands for costly care largely due to their suffering from often preventable diseases (heart disease, diabetes, dementia, obesity, etc.) These diseases are often caused by poor lifestyle choice.

What has influenced me lately?

1. "The New Mediterranean Diet Cookbook by Nancy Harmon Jenkins
2. the Aspen Brain Institutes series on food and the brain, which includes advice on food preparation
3. Jon Gabriel

4. Bob Roth and his twice-daily TM meditations on Zoom or calls and his book "Strength in Silence." There are many types of good meditations but I particularly like TM and Thicht Nhat Hahns' walking meditation and his book "Savor"
5. Pastor Rick Warrens' book about health and weight "The Daniel Plan" with the help of Dr. Mark Hyman, Dr. Daniel Amen and Dr. Oz.
6. Tiffany Cruikshanks' book "Meditate Your Weight."
7. Pastor Rick Warrens' book …."The Purpose Driven Life"
8. David Jackson and his website and sometimes TV show "Food Over 50"

There are more influences but these are what came to mind today. I truly believe that as more and more people lack good/or any food, clothing, shelter and transportation we run the risk of becoming a third-world nation. I hope our investment in others well-being and the investment of some of our time can make the difference, saving us from 'evil.'

The Carnivorous Mushrooms

A scream…a dream…step out of the dream
Too much partying…everyone was excited about the coming day
Too much cider and wine
She didn't drink because alcohol was toxic to her brain.
She rubbed her hands across her forehead
Even in her dreams she was schizophrenic, down to the core of her being….
Squish! Crunch!
She looked down at her feet which had obliterated a mushroom
Gracious! There are mushrooms everywhere…

> Mushrooms…pickled, pickling in my brain
> They come out after the rain
> When the sky is gray, full of wet
> Oh, so pretty, how they get.
> Caps of white, caps of brown
> They also get an olive hue….Woo Hoo!
> Stalks so thin have nutrients within
> Flavors lodged within.

She contemplated, in a Zen-like frame of mind, what she saw below her on the ground. Myriads of mushrooms. It made her hungry just to look at them…

> Waking up from a deep, deep sleep
> Into my mouth there did creep the aroma…
> Subtle, perfection…gobble, gobble
> Misty gray the day, misty white waiting for the light
>   Of the sun whose rays pour down
> Wilting the mushrooms springing from the ground.
> For those less timorous than she
> What a dinner there will be
> Portobello, what a fellow, causes my teeth to clack
> Gobble it down, down the back….of my throat…

I'm excited, more than usual. To begin with Joe Biden gave his address to the nation to celebrate this auspicious occasion. It filled me with hope for our future and it fills me with a deep appreciation for his kindness, compassion and competence. With help from Above he and Kamala Harris may be able to bring us back from the depths of the pandemic which has engulfed us.

Most of my family are either dead or have disowned Russell and me because of differences in political opinions. Our friends are far away, involved with their own families, in quarantine or simply uneasy about going out because of covid. Therefore it will just be the two of us celebrating. Even so I am thrilled and excited.

I decided to celebrate by attempting a Thanksgiving dinner for two, using a chicken instead of a huge turkey. Also charred sweet potatoes with honey butter, a salad of pico d' gallo, diced onions and mushrooms (subtle and perfect to gobble) and marinated olives. For those of you who don't have as much free time as me since I'm retired, the salad is made from pre-diced tomatoes and onions which come in a container from the store plus mushrooms which I dice. They are tasty, no added ingredients and relatively inexpensive. If you equate time with money they're actually cheaper.

Even so it took me nearly 1 ½ hours to get the preparation done. Russell wanted to eat at 5:00 pm so I had to get started cooking around 2:30. "Why?" you may ask am I so fanatic about wanting to learn to cook. Possibly because so many of my friends, family and acquaintances have died prematurely and unkindly…. possibly because they didn't physically and mentally move and their horrid eating habits could have led to their untimely and miserable passing.

Many people today, especially those with less affluence, live in areas called "food deserts", and don't have access or money for decent food, and lacking insurance they are at higher risk to die from covid (my opinion.)

Therefore it seems important to me to celebrate this special day by giving thanks to God for all His kindnesses and mercy to me and those I care about. I pray He helps us as a nation to cease the hatred that has nearly destroyed us, and to realize we need to make the changes necessary to restore sanity to our society and the planet. It seems that life as we have known it is gone (change is inevitable) and we should work towards an even better future. Bless us and Happy Holiday to one and all.

Food and Water to Drink Help Ones' Brain to Think

Avocados are the best, better than much of the rest for good fats
Which we need…indeed
They fill the body and mind and soul so we don't overeat
I repeat----we don't overeat
One of the 7 Deadly Sins is gluttony ending in diabesity---
No longer a mystery.

Delgado squash is good, stuffed with protein, if you would
The skin is delicious and nutritious so chew away
Alvin gets it once a year when in the garden it does appear
You'll need a farmer to provide it for you…that is true.

Berries fill the being with seeing…light steps to take
As granulated sugar you forsake
Frozen or fresh they pass the test, they taste swell as well
Spread over whole-milk yogurt sweetened with honey
They make a good dessert costing little money

Water of course should be your choice
It hydrates your tissues preventing dire issues
Of dehydration and dis-ease
Give me lots of water please.

There are many more good foods to eat….they're 'real'
And not processed, or should I say 'messed.'
So enjoy your food, it's fun and good.

Covid-19 is raging and I hope to help by writing about learning to cook and eat for good health and to help our immune systems. I don't know whether it is the aftermath of the 20th Century (World Wars 1 and 2, the Great Depression) or the resulting affluence and lack of movement, but our eating habits and foods are not doing us any favors…nor the rest of the world to whom we are spreading our unhealthy and unsavory foods… based on chemicals, sugars, poisonous trans-fats, heavy doses of salt, etc.

When I was growing up during World War 2 the great availability and variety of unusual foods was not available. Food was (to my family) sparse and often monotonous, basically what we grew in the backyard and what the local farmers could provide. There was not a lot of food to be had so we were not so fat. Cars were not prevalent and we walked and skated and even biked if our parents could afford bicycles.

Today huge subsidies are paid to farmers to raise wheat, corn and soy which are used in ways unhealthy for humans, animals and the environment. These products are used largely to feed animals in 'factory farms', feeding them food alien to their natures, using huge amounts of precious water and spoiling the soil and air. I am appalled at the conditions in which these animals are kept. I was a vegan/vegetarian for years and overweight because I worried about these animals. When I added animal protein (Genesis 9:1-4)the excess pounds melted away and I am healthier and more active than most of my peers as is my brother (we are in our late 70's) Although God okayed meat for us to eat He never intended us to treat animals and poultry inhumanely as our 'factory farms' do. As for the subsidies….they should be going to help farmers raise fruits and veggies and animals in their natural environment… to bring us good health and attractive bodies and sound minds.

Hopefully those of us who are learning to prepare nutritious foods and not lots of them will be able to eat soundly. As for me, I eat what I want when I want it. For instance, last night I fixed spaghetti and meatballs and salad, then a small slice of fruitcake which Claxton prepares during the holiday season. I prepared the spaghetti from Raos' prepared sauce and used organic spaghetti, adding frozen meatballs, garlic and black olives, sprinkling parmesan cheese over it before serving. I checked the ingredient label and there was only food in the jar. I have noticed when the producers use good food they make the labels readable. When they use junk and lots of it the labels are almost, if not, impossible to read.

It is imperative that these healthy foods be made possible for those less fortunate to obtain and eat. If what I am learning is true (and I believe it is) our food affects the ability of our brains to function properly and intelligently and for our physical bodies to be healthy, attractive and active.

When I Sing Happy

When I sing happy the shadows are lifted from my eyes
As they glance towards the skies
Where the clouds go flying by…so high! So high!
When the bars are lifted from my soul
Which by now is growing old, growing cold and ready to depart
To where my treasure is, and I will never depart
From the place in space where I will never be in disgrace.
Where there is a place inside of me, free and full of glee
Laughing, dancing, singing all day long
Where my bones are once again strong
Where my third eye can peer into the haze
Undefeated in its' gaze
Where Jesus teaches me not to be full of distrust, anger, hate and ire
Where He teaches me to extinguish the fire
And love my neighbors as they are….

The brain is affected by more than only food. Consider: faith, prayer and meditation, exercise and movement, new and interesting challenges, rest and diminished stress, the society and friendship and love of ones' fellow human beings and other creatures. There are probably more but for now that is enough. Let's consider some of these:

1.…exercise and movement because they stimulate the heart and the brain and the body, all of whom say "thanks." My favorite exercise is walking which I have done since a young child. I stroll and admire the breeze, the sun and moon and stars, the animals and birds, and trees. When I was younger dancing was another beloved form of movement. I danced from the 2nd grade until I was in my 50s' and could no longer find dance for adults where I live. How sad! Not only is dancing fun but it is a wonderful form of creative expression of the beauty of life in all of its manifestations. Yoga is almost as much fun. Forms of movement on TV include Mary Ann Wilsons' 'Sit and be Fit,' 'Body Electric,' Wai-Lanas' Yoga, Miranda Esmond-Whites' Classical Stretch. There are many types for the different types of people who like different types of movement. One of the advantages of walking is that the brain loves to be outdoors in nature and sunlight. I also love walking at night in the dark but that is probably not advisable. It is wonderful to feel the sun, feel the breezes and the sun warming ones bones and entering the brain through the eyes.

I am not so good at sitting and enjoy walking meditation in my room, pacing back and forth contemplating what I have just read in my Bible. This is as much fun as is rocking back and forth in my rocking chair. Thicht Nhat Hahn likes this form of meditation. The mind wanders and explores, observing life as it unfolds before ones 'mind and eyes. It's difficult to stress when moving. Movement seems to dissipate the presence of stress and helps to rid one of un-ease.

Many people like more lively, cardio forms of movement which are also good. Running is satisfying to many but most likely hard on the joints. Bicycling is wonderful, probably having no peer. My brother biked across the USA from the Pacific to the Atlantic in his 60s…over the Rockies. WOW! What an adventure and he especially loved how much he could eat. Swimming is an amazing form of exercise…rhythmic and lengthening and good for the breath. Movement is fun! I could go on and on but you get the point.

I hope you enjoyed your holiday season….Christmas, Kwanzai, Hannaka and any unknown to me. I hope you got to see the conjunction of Jupiter and Saturn celebrating the Winter Solstice on December 21, 2020.

Food Has the Power to Heal

If I could see beyond the shadows to the light from above
Then I would be healed by Your love so kind
Helping to encourage my mind.
Being down in my head made me wish to be dead….
Gone, gone, gone….alone, alone, alone…..still, still, still,
Heavy as a stone…a gray, heavy rock
Incapable of shock!
Do I wonder as I wander?
What is tormenting me?
Is it weight, is it hate! Causing such consternation
Such desperation to my being incapable of seeing?

I am taking a brief moment to lament the state of the country right now, especially as most of us are upset about what is going on with covid and political insecurity. These problems arealso aggravated by food and shelter insecurity which has become commonplace affecting adults, young people and children. This concerns me for 2 reasons:

1. People need good food not only to live but to prosper intellectually, spiritually, and physically. Starvation is especially traumatic for children. When I was sick I was also severely anorexic and when I got to the hospital I weighed around 20 pounds less than I do now, no food had passed my lips for days. I was starving and didn't care. Yes! Starving! I didn't care! The doctor said "Miss Goin, you must eat or die!" Starving is no fun and surprisingly when I contemplated an early demise I realized I wasn't ready to pass on to the Great Beyond. So I started to eat.

Do we really want millions of our citizens to starve to death? Does God want this for us? I think not. At the same time millions more are sick from obesity and the ensuing health problems. At this time in the world there are probably as many people starving as are eating themselves to death. Neither is desirable or healthy.

2. As a nation we need our citizens to have good food to be healthy, happy and productive….not sick, unable to think or concentrate and also not to be fat (which if I understand correctly causes the brain to be relatively smaller.) One thing I do know: Sharon at the Fauquier Community Thrift Bank Food Store told me that every $1 donated will buy $4 worth of food and water. Some of the churches are having food drives but the need is inestimable. If we are fortunate enough to have jobs or money we need to share. And sharing doesn't mean soft drinks and junk food, fast food, and heavily processed 'food-like substances.' One of my favorite verses in the Bible is Romans 12:13…."distributing to the needs of the saints, given to hospitality." It pretty well sums up what I believe about my reason for being and having so much.

I don't have much money but God has mercifully seen to it that I have what I need, and it is important to Him that I share and use what is available to me wisely, which is fun….and fun is important to me and most people I know.

When Your Stomach is Hollow

Thus ends my book on how and why to cook
With fun and merriment making your stomach and brain content
Recipes will (in another book) follow for when your stomach is hollow.

As down the gullet food makes its way
Fueling us for the present day, tasting good in every way.
I learned from flying that dinner is not complete
Without a touch of something 'sweet'.
Fruit and yogurt with honey will often do
When dinner is through.
But not so much that your brain will complain….
Too much sugar is not sane.

After nearly three months of being unable to write because of what is going on in our country I finally decided to end this book . Although I foresee many difficulties in the future of our countryI now am seeing hope, which hopefully is not an illusion. It's the Sunday after Easter and my Easter dinner for 7 was really good. I used a wonderful recipe from the current Bon Appetit… a recipe for Beef Wellington with Green Sauce which took Deb and me almost three hours to bring to fruition. We served it with scalloped potatoes, macaroni and cheese, broiled asparagus with parmesan cheese, and roasted carrots….followed by Key Lime Pie and fruit and yogurt sweetened with honey (my favorite.) It was yummy!

One important thing aspiring cooks must remember is to chop and measure everything before starting the actual recipe. My next dinner will be bar-b-que short ribs with cole slaw, scalloped potatoes and something else. I am preparing so much 'soul fool' so as to accommodate my brother who is having difficulty right now not feeling so good. This dinner will be to celebrate Debs husband Michaels birthday which should be a riotous good time.

Alvin is getting fresh vegetables for the spring. They are wonderful and fresh and full of good things for the psyche. They are also reasonably priced which is important. The Methodist Church in my neighborhood is providing free food for those needing it once a month. For rich people these times seem to be good but for the rest of us money is not so available and we need to be thoughtful and careful shoppers, assuming one is not in a food desert.

I have babbled enough about the problems associated with excess weight physically and emotionally and am happy to say that for myself, most of my remaining old friends and my new friends excess weight is not an issue. We all eat carefully and prepare our food which I am having fun learning to do.

Don't forget:

1. Thank God for your daily bread
2. Hydrate, hydrate, hydrate!

3. Treat our planet with respect and love
4. Treat our fellow humans and other creatures with respect and love.
5. Luke 14: 13-14…..”But when you give a feast, invite the poor, the maimed, the lame, the blind and you will be blessed because they cannot repay you; for you shall be repaid at the resurrection of the just.”
6. be kind to and love yourself.

And this verse sums it all up:

Here with a Loaf of Bread beneath the Bough,
A Flask of Wine, a Book of Verse-and Thou
Beside me singing in the Wilderness-
And Wilderness is Paradise enow.

From the Rubaiyat of Omar Khayayam
Rendered in English verse by Edward Fitzgerald

The END

Printed in the United States
by Baker & Taylor Publisher Services